Canadian Brass

Christmas Tradition

7 Arrangements for Brass Quintet

Created for and Recorded by The Canadian Brass
www.canadianbrass.com

Cover art: Robyn McCallum

Recorded by The Canadian Brass on:
1 Christmas Tradition (Opening Day Recordings)
2 The Christmas Album (Philips)
3 Sweet Songs of Christmas (Opening Day Recordings)

ISBN 978-1-4234-6381-8

THE CANADIAN
BRASS

DISTRIBUTED BY

HAL•LEONARD®
CORPORATION

7777 W. BLUEMOUND RD. P.O. BOX 13819 MILWAUKEE, WI 53213

Visit Hal Leonard Online at
www.halleonard.com

F Horn

Canadian Brass Collection

Away in a Manger

from *The Christmas Album* (CD: 426 835 - 4)

W. J. Kirkpatrick
Arranged by Stephen McNeff

Simple, Chorale-like

♩ = 69-72

Music preparation by
Richard Maslove

Canadian Brass Collection

Deck the Halls - In Dulci Jubilo

from *Christmas Tradition* (CD : ODR 7345)

Andante ♩= 92

Arranged by Eric N. Robertson

Music preparation by Richard Maslove

6 **F Horn**

Canadian Brass Collection

Grand Angelic March

from *Christmas Tradition* (CD: ODR 7345)

Eric N. Robertson

Music preparartion by
Richard Maslove

Canadian Brass Collection
Jolly Old St. Nicholas
from *Christmas Tradition* (CD: ODR 7345)

Arranged by Arthur Frackenpohl
Adapted by Tony Rickard

Music preparation by
Tony Rickard and Richard Maslove

Canadian Brass Collection

Sweet Songs of Christmas

from *Sweet Songs of Christmas* (CD: ODR 9328)

Christopher Dedrick

Music preparation by
Richard Maslove

Canadian Brass Collection

We Three Kings of Orient Are

from *The Christmas Album* (CD: 426 835 - 4)

J.H. Hopkins
Arranged by Stephen McNeff

Music preparation by
Richard Maslove

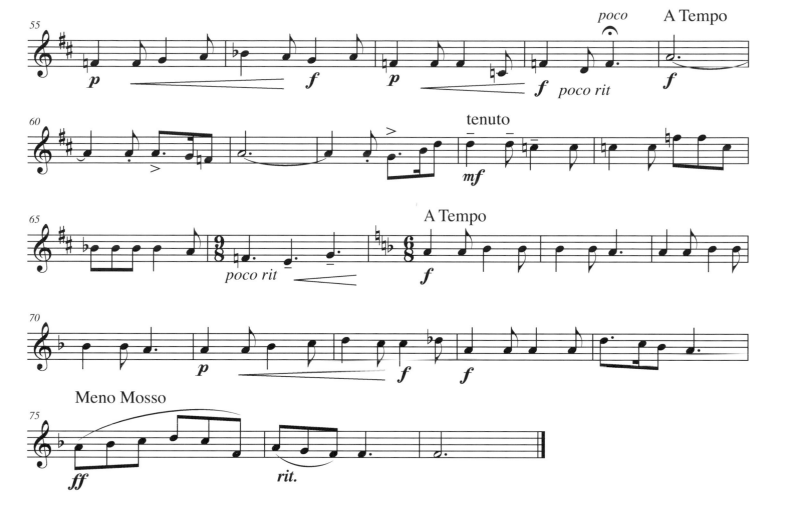

Canadian Brass Collection

Dance of the Sugar Plum Fairy

Andante non troppo   from *The Christmas Album* (CD: 426 835 - 4)

P. Tschaikovsky
Arranged by Stephen McNeff

Music preparation by Richard Maslove